Copic

Coloring Guide™

Level 2: Nature

LET YOURSELF GO
You're Bound to Bloom

D1332275

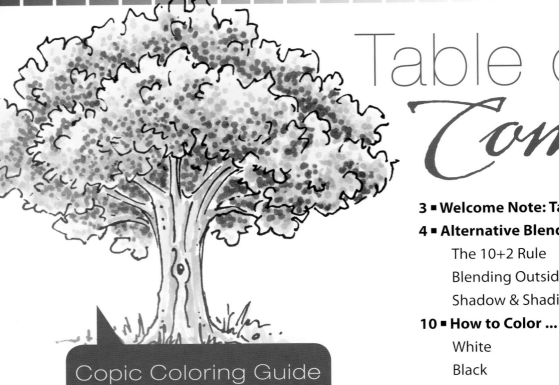

Copic Coloring Guide
Level 2: Nature

EDITOR Tanya Fox
ART DIRECTOR Brad Snow
PUBLISHING SERVICES DIRECTOR Brenda Gallmeyer
MANAGING EDITOR Brooke Smith
GRAPHIC DESIGNER Nick Pierce
COPY SUPERVISOR Deborah Morgan
COPY EDITORS Emily Carter, Rebecca Detwiler
TECHNICAL EDITOR Corene Painter
PHOTOGRAPHY SUPERVISOR Tammy Christian
PHOTO STYLISTS Tammy Liechty, Tammy Steiner
PHOTOGRAPHY Matthew Owen
PRODUCTION ARTIST SUPERVISOR Erin Brandt
PRODUCTION ARTIST Nicole Gage
PRODUCTION ASSISTANTS Marj Morgan, Judy Neuenschwander

ISBN: 978-1-59635-409-8
Printed in the USA
1 2 3 4 5 6 7 8 9

Table of Contents

Taking It to the *Next Level*

Marianne and I were humbled by the excitement and support we received for our first book, **Copic Coloring Guide**. THANK YOU! We've heard your plea for MORE tutorials, MORE techniques and MORE inspiration—thus, the series continues!

Our goal as educators is to give you the tools necessary to strengthen your knowledge, boost your confidence and take your skills to the next level. In this book, we focus on more advanced blending tips and techniques and answer some of the most commonly asked, "How do you color (fill in the blank) …" questions.

As a bonus, we have included a CD containing all of the hand-drawn images used in the tutorial section so you can print them and practice right along with us. And in order to provide you with larger, more detailed photos and full coloring instructions for each project, we have placed the assembly instructions for the projects on the CD as well.

It is our hope that the enclosed tips and tutorials will not only prompt you to try new things, but that they become the basis for your very own experimentation and color exploration. These tips and techniques are just the starting point. Learn them, practice them and make them your own.

—*Colleen and Marianne*

> *Actually, all education is self-education. A teacher is only a guide, to point out the way, and no school, no matter how excellent, can give you education. What you receive is like the outlines in a child's coloring book. You must fill in the colors yourself.*
>
> —*Louis L'Amour*

Alternative *Blending & Shading* Groups

There are a number of ways to color images. In the *Copic® Coloring Guide*, we covered how to read the Copic numbering system and how to select good blending groups based on some basic rules. In the following section, we show how to break those rules and give some guidelines for picking alternative blending and shading groups.

Blending Beyond the Code

When beginning with Copic markers, you are taught to pick blending groups with the same letter (color family), same first number (saturation), and two or three digits difference in the last number (shade/value). Here is an example of an image colored following those basic rules. The following markers were used: B000, B00, B02, B04, BV000, BV00, BV02, BV04, R46.

While this is good, images can be made even more realistic by changing the saturation as well as the shade. By going one or two steps less saturated with each marker, you can create more believable contrast and shading.

Some basic things to know about shadows and shading

- *Shadows are not only darker in shade, but also less saturated. This means they are not as vibrant and typically have more gray in them.*

- *Shadows are often cooler in tone.*

- *Objects in the foreground are more vibrant than objects in the background.*

The 10+2 Rule

$$B00 + 10 = B10 + 2 = B12 + 10 = B22 + 2 = B24$$

Here is an example of the 10+2 Rule:

Materials

White smooth cardstock
Tropical fish digital stamp
Markers: B000, B00, B12, B24, BV00, BV11, BV23, R46
Computer with printer

B00 is the base color.

Step 1: Pick a beginning color. This should be a light shade in the color family you want to work with. For example, the fish is based in B00 and B000 is worked in as the light color.

B00+10+2=B12

Step 2: Pick a medium shade marker in the same color family but with one digit less saturation. By adding 10 + 2 to the beginning marker number, you will find a usable blend. In the example, B12 is feathered into the fish.

Remember—the first digit goes UP as the saturation goes DOWN.

Step 3: Following the same general rule, pick a darker shade, again with one or two digits less saturation. For example, B24 is added as final shading on fish.

This will give your shading more depth and a realistic appeal.

B12+10+2=B24

Sources: *White smooth X-Press It Blending Card and markers from Imagination International Inc.; digital stamp by Marianne Walker from included CD.*

Remember, the 10+2 Rule is a guideline and can be tweaked to work for you.

Blending Outside the Color Family

To take your coloring even further, you can completely leave the rules behind and move outside the color family for blends. This allows you to create beautiful undertones and interesting color combinations.

Here is an example of Blending Outside the Color Family:

Materials

White smooth cardstock
Tropical fish digital stamp
Markers: R46, Y11, Y15, YR15, YR18
Computer with printer

Step 1: Base the entire image in a light color to create an undertone. The example uses Y11.

Step 4: Feather in a darker shade of the same color. The example uses YR18.

Step 5: Jump to a different color family and add the darkest shade to some areas. The example uses R46 on fins and tail.

Sources: White smooth X-Press It Blending Card and markers from Imagination International Inc.; digital stamp by Marianne Walker from included CD.

Here are a few tips to keep in mind

- *Colors next to each other on the color wheel are much easier to blend and look more natural together.*

- *While colors don't need to be the same saturation, try to keep them similar (within 3–4 digits) for a more cohesive look.*

Step 2: Feather in a darker shade of the same color. The example uses Y15.

Step 3: Add a similar shade in a different color family. The example uses YR15.

Shadow & Shading Options

Sometimes there isn't a color dark enough or desaturated enough to give eye-popping contrast in the shadows. In this situation, there are two options and the following example shows both styles.

Complementary Color Shadow & Shading

One of the "rules" for shadows is that they are less saturated, which often means that they are grayer. When two complementary colors are mixed together (red/green, blue/orange, yellow/purple), they create gray. Adding a complementary color is a perfect way to create dark shaded areas and crisp cast shadows.

Gray Shadow & Shading

Adding a touch of gray is another simple way to create those deep shadows. Remember that shadows are typically cooler, so you probably want to pull from the Cool Gray markers for this. It takes a bit of practice to find just the right shade of gray to use; too light and it will lighten your image and too dark will look unnatural. My favorite shading gray is C3, but make sure to test your own color combinations and keep them in your sketchbook.

Materials

White smooth cardstock
Giraffe digital stamp
Markers: BV02, C3, E33, E50, E51, Y21, YR14, YR24, W1, W3, W5
Computer with printer

Notice that the basic blending and shading is completed with normal color combinations, and the complementary color, or gray, is only added as a final touch.

Step 1: Base entire image with E50. Feather E51 onto image for light shading.

Step 2: Add darker shading to giraffe with E33 and blend.

Step 3: Color spots with YR21, YR24 and YR14. Color hooves with W1, W3 and W5.

On the traditional 12-step color wheel, blue-violet is a complement or opposite of yellow-red.

Step 4: Add touches of BV02 (a complementary color) to areas that would be darkest and as cast shadows.

Sources: *White smooth X-Press It Blending Card and markers from Imagination International Inc.; digital stamp by Marianne Walker from included CD.*

As a second option for creating cast shadows, add touches of C3 to shade with gray.

How to *Color* ...

One of the most common questions we get as instructors is, "How do I color (fill in the blank)?" While there are no hard-and-fast rules to coloring specific objects, there are some general guidelines to follow. In this section, we cover some of the most common topics we get asked about.

White

Some people leave white objects uncolored. While this is generally OK, it's not the most effective way to color white. Unlike black, you actually use different colors to represent white.

Tips and Tricks

- *Highlights in white objects often reflect the color of the light source.*
- *Shadows on white objects often reflect the color of the surface the object is resting on.*
- *Smooth and man-made objects often have cool colors for shading.*
- *Be careful with grays as shading for white. Grays have a tendency to make an object appear dirty or unnatural.*
- *You can set off a white object by coloring the background.*

Materials

White smooth cardstock
Sweet Sheep digital stamp
Markers: E30, E70, G05, G24, G40, RV66, RV91, W3, Y28, YR08, YR20
Colorless Blender (0)
Computer with printer

Step 3: Add more shadows with a darker tone (Y28).

Step 4: Blend using either the lighter shade or another light shade in a different tone. Y20 was used here to create a nice golden tone.

Step 6: Using a juicy Colorless Blender and small circles, push the color back into the shadows.

Natural textures or living objects often have warm colors for shading.

Step 1: Decide whether your white object will have warm or cool shading and what color any highlights will be.

Step 2: Base the shadows only with the lightest color (E30). Go further into the white area than the finished shading will actually be.

Step 5: Add a touch of complementary color to more heavily shaded areas (RV91 and E70).

Step 7: Add cast shadows and subtle highlights with W3.

Sources: White smooth X-Press It Blending Card, markers and Colorless Blender from Imagination International Inc.; digital stamp by Marianne Walker from included CD.

Black

Black is never just black. Not only are there many shades of black, there are also different tones. Black can be either warm or cool. If black is warm, it has brown undertones, and if it is cool, it typically has blue undertones. Copic grays are wonderful for coloring black. Use W grays or T grays for warm blacks and C grays for cool blacks. Of course, if you don't want either tone, remain neutral with the N grays.

Keep in mind that black is a color like any other, and you will want a variety of values to create highlights and shadows.

Materials
White smooth cardstock
Little Black Bug digital stamp
Markers: C1, C3, C5, C7, C9
Computer with printer

Step 2: Base the image with a light gray (C3). Leave the highlighted area uncolored.

Leave your highlights white or add them in with Opaque White pigment paint.

Step 1: Pick three to five grays in the same tones. Typically, every other shade is sufficient. This sample is colored using cool grays.

Step 3: Add shading with a medium gray (C5) and blend.

Step 4: Add more shading with a dark gray (C7) and blend.

Step 5: Add a touch of C9 to the deepest shaded areas.

Step 6: Blend highlight out gently with a light shade of gray (C1).

Sources: *White smooth X-Press It Blending Card and markers from Imagination International Inc.; digital stamp by Marianne Walker from included CD.*

Tips and Tricks
- *Add cast shadows with a very dark blue (B39, B99) or dark brown (E79).*
- *Shiny or reflective surfaces (like patent leather) will have LOTS of contrast.*
- *Be careful when using the Colorless Blender. It can intensify the brown or blue tone in the color.*

Foliage

Forget smooth coloring and soft blends. When coloring foliage it's important to identify details and create texture.

The techniques for adding this texture are dotting and/or scribbling.

Materials

White smooth cardstock
Old Oak digital stamp
Markers: E13, E17, E30, G29, G82, G85,
  YG21, YG23, YG25
Computer with printer

Step 3: Pick two to three markers that are darker and/or less saturated than the base colors. No need to follow rules for blending groups here (G82, G85, G29).

Tips and Tricks

- **Do NOT blend the scribbles or dots.**
- **Vary the size of the dots for more interest.**

Instead of creating scribbles, try adding each color by dotting with the tip of the brush nib.

Step 1: Identify the basic shape of the foliage. Is the tree or plant a circle, cylinder, cone, sphere or a combination of shapes? This tree is made up of a number of spheres.

Keep your wrist and fingers loose to create carefree scribbles.

Step 4: Using the lightest shade, make loose scribbles over the entire surface.

Do not cover all of the lightest color, even in the shaded areas.

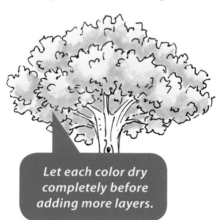

Let each color dry completely before adding more layers.

Step 2: Color each individual shape as normal with a basic blending group. This will become your undertone (YG21, YG23, YG25).

Step 5: Using the medium shade, make loose scribbles to add slight shading.

Step 6: Using the darkest shade, make loose scribbles to add shadows.

Sources: *White smooth X-Press It Blending Card and markers from Imagination International Inc.; digital stamp by Marianne Walker from included CD.*

Coloring Rocks

Rocks, pebbles and stones come in all shapes and sizes, and there are many different ways to color them. Here is a basic tutorial to get you started.

Materials

White smooth cardstock
Solid as a Rock digital stamp
Markers: N1, N3, N5, R22, YG63, YG67
Computer with printer

Step 1: Color smaller parts of the image that might be in the foreground or in front of the rocks.

Step 2: Base the rocks with a light neutral color (N1).

Tips and Tricks

- *Add dots of varying sizes and colors to the rock shadows to add texture.*
- *Lightly dab the rock with the Colorless Blender to create a mottled appearance.*

Step 3: While the base coat is still wet, feather in a darker shade from the bottom by flicking toward the light source (N3).

Step 4: Using a darker shade (N5), feather more color toward the light source in an irregular pattern.

Step 5: Blend only slightly, leaving irregularities, lumps and bumps.

Sources: White smooth X-Press It Blending Card and markers from Imagination International Inc.; digital stamp by Marianne Walker from included CD.

Ground

It is important to "ground" your images (giving them something to sit or stand on) otherwise they look as if they are floating in mid-air. Here is just one way to create ground for your image. Play around with this technique and adapt it to fit your image and style.

Materials

White smooth cardstock
Solid as a Rock digital stamp
Markers: BG11, BG93, E42, E43, N1, N3, N5, R22, YG63, YG67
Colorless Blender (0)
Computer with printer

Step 1: Color your image as normal.

Step 2: Pick colors that represent the type of ground the image is on and possibly some colors from the image itself.

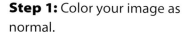

Step 3: Feather two colors out from the base of the image. This can be done roughly and blending isn't necessary (N3, E42).

Step 4: With a juicy Colorless Blender, start in the white area and push the color back toward the image. Do not over blend; remove the streaks from the edges only.

Step 5: Let the ground dry completely. Add irregular-sized dots of two or three coordinating colors (E43, N3, BG93).

Step 6: Let dry completely. Add dots with the Colorless Blender.

Step 7: Add darker cast shadows near the bottom of the image and add a background if wanted.

Sources: *White smooth X-Press It Blending Card, markers and Colorless Blender from Imagination International Inc.; digital stamp by Marianne Walker from included CD.*

Fur

Loveable, huggable, fuzzy little friends deserve special treatment! While you can use the scribbling or dotting technique to create the look of fur, here are two more techniques to create that fuzzy fleece.

Sponging

Sponging creates darker fur than other techniques.

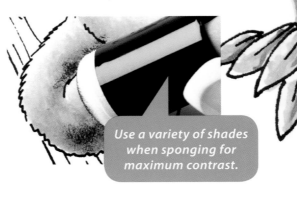

> **Mask off any area you don't want inked.**

> **Use a variety of shades when sponging for maximum contrast.**

Step 1: Color the fur as normal (N0, N2, N4). Create mask for tree and mask tree if needed.

Step 3: Quickly dab the sponge onto colored image using lighter shades as you move toward the highlights.

Step 4: Repeat steps 2 and 3 as necessary.

Step 2: Scribble ink onto a sponge or piece of cloth (N6).

Step 5: Remove masks and color the rest of the image as normal.

Materials

White smooth cardstock
Masking material (optional)
Koala Hugs digital stamp
Markers: E17, E21, E34, E47, G24, G28, N0,
   N2, N4, N6, YG21
Colorless Blender (0)
Sponge
Computer with printer

Sources: White smooth X-Press It Blending Card, markers and Colorless Blender from Imagination International Inc.; digital stamp by Marianne Walker from included CD.

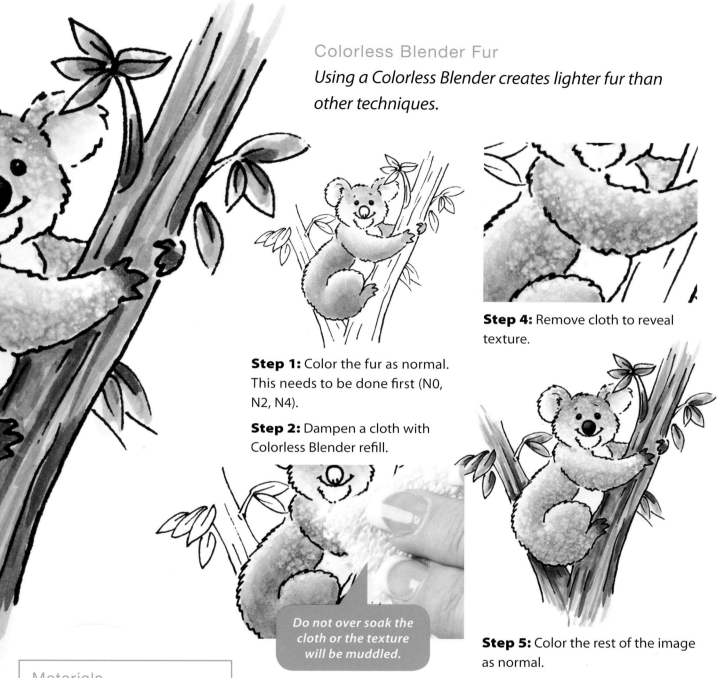

Colorless Blender Fur

Using a Colorless Blender creates lighter fur than other techniques.

Step 4: Remove cloth to reveal texture.

Step 1: Color the fur as normal. This needs to be done first (N0, N2, N4).

Step 2: Dampen a cloth with Colorless Blender refill.

Do not over soak the cloth or the texture will be muddled.

Step 3: Place dampened cloth over colored image and hold for a few seconds. Do not press or squeeze.

Step 5: Color the rest of the image as normal.

Sources: *White smooth X-Press It Blending Card, markers and Colorless Blender refill from Imagination International Inc.; digital stamp by Marianne Walker from included CD.*

Materials

White smooth cardstock
Masking material (optional)
Koala Hugs digital stamp
Markers: E17, E21, E34, E47, G24, G28, N0, N2, N4, N6, YG21
Colorless Blender (0)
Cloth
Computer with printer

Tips and Tricks

- *Use a variety of surfaces to create different textures.*
- *Let the image dry completely before using the Colorless Blender for crisper texture.*

Flowers

There are thousands of types of flowers and just about as many ways to color them! Here is a simple way to color flowers that form in bunches or bundles.

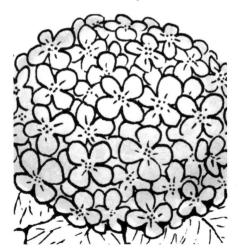

Materials

White smooth cardstock
Hydrangea digital stamp
Markers: BV000, BV00, BV01, BV02, BV23, BV25, G24, V01, V06, YG03, YG11, YG17
Computer with printer

Step 1: Identify the basic shape of the flower bunch. Is it a circle, cylinder, cone or sphere? The hydrangea image is an example of a sphere.

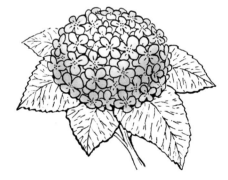

Step 2: Color, blend and shade the entire shape as normal with any blending group. Don't try to tackle individual flowers; just focus on the shape of the whole bunch (BV000, BV00, BV01, BV02).

Step 3 (optional): Apply a light coordinating color to the highlighted area to give a more natural appearance (V01).

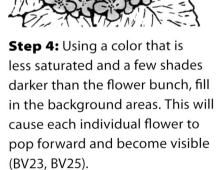

Step 4: Using a color that is less saturated and a few shades darker than the flower bunch, fill in the background areas. This will cause each individual flower to pop forward and become visible (BV23, BV25).

Step 5: Add details to the flower centers and color foliage to complete the image.

Sources: *White smooth X-Press It Blending Card and markers from Imagination International Inc.; digital stamp by Marianne Walker from included CD.*

Wood

You can create a number of wood-like looks with just a few simple flicks of color.

Step 1: Begin with the lightest shade (E33). Always color in the direction of the wood grain. Flick color from the edges toward the middle so the color is darker and more solid near the edges.

Materials

White smooth cardstock
Sign Post digital stamp
Markers: E33, E37, E47, YG63, YG67, RV34
Computer with printer

Step 2: Add streaks of a medium shade (E37) by flicking from the edges toward the center. Do not cover all of the light color. Do not blend.

Step 3: Using the tip of the brush nib, add streaks of the darkest shade (E47). Flick from the edges toward the center. Do not blend.

Step 4: Color the rest of the image.

Sources: White smooth X-Press It Blending Card and markers from Imagination International Inc.; digital stamp by Marianne Walker from included CD.

Metal

While metal comes in a variety of colors, we are going to focus on silvery metal objects like silver, pewter and platinum.

Materials

White smooth cardstock
Milk Can digital stamp
Markers: C3, C5, C7
Computer with printer

Step 1: Following the shape of the object, add a base coat of the lightest color (C3). Keep your highlights white.

Step 3: Add the darkest gray (C7) to the darkest shadow areas. Notice the layers are unblended.

Step 5: Blend the medium shade into the light shade with the light color.

Step 2: Again, following the shape of the object, add a layer of medium gray for shading (C5).

Step 4: Working backward from dark to light, blend the dark into the medium shade with the medium color.

Step 6: Blend the lightest shade into white with the colorless blender.

Tips and Tricks

- *New or shiny metal will have a very reflective surface. It will have crisp blends and areas of high contrast.*
- *Older, dull or galvanized metal will have softer blends and less contrast.*
- *Always color following the shape of the object.*
- *Cool grays look more natural than warm grays.*

Sources: *White smooth X-Press It Blending Card and markers from Imagination International Inc.; digital stamp by Marianne Walker from included CD.*

Sky

Like grounding, creating a sky gives your image someplace to rest and helps set it apart from the background.

Materials

White smooth cardstock
Sky Bird digital stamp
Markers: B32, E42, N2, Y38
Colorless Blender (0)
Computer with printer

Tips and Tricks

- *Use a variety of colors for different effects.*

- *Try using this technique around stamped images to create a fade-to-white effect.*

Step 1: Color the entire image as normal.

Try pre-saturating an area slightly outside the image with the Colorless Blender to help blend the flick when first applying the sky.

Step 2: Using a color that is just slightly darker than you want your finished sky to be, flick from the image outward. The longer your flicks, the larger your finished sky area will be.

Be careful not to push color into the actual image.

Step 3: Using a very juicy Colorless Blender and small circles, push the color back toward the image. Don't stop or you may get streaks. As you push the color, a dark area may build up. Be careful to hide this under the stamped line.

Step 4: Continue working with the blender around the entire image until all of the blue is softened and blended smoothly to white.

Sources: *White smooth X-Press It Blending Card, markers and Colorless Blender from Imagination International Inc.; digital stamp by Marianne Walker from included CD.*

Materials

White smooth cardstock
Puddles the Duck digital stamp
Markers: B32, B34, B37, W1, W3, Y11, Y17
Computer with printer

Water

Coloring water can be intimidating, but with a few simple steps you will have colorful ponds, rivers and puddles.

Step 1: Color all other parts of the image first.

Step 2: Add a base coat of light blue to the water (B32). Keep ripples and highlights white.

Step 3: Darken the edges of the puddle and the shadow of the image with a medium color (B34).

Step 4: Darken the very edges of the puddle and the shadow with the darkest shade (B37).

Streaks are okay as long as they are in the same direction as the flow of the water or ripples.

Step 5: Lightly blend. Leave some streaks to represent ripples.

Step 6: Add reflections by streaking in the same color as the object being reflected.

Sources: *White smooth X-Press It Blending Card and markers from Imagination International Inc.; digital stamp by Marianne Walker from included CD.*

Tips and Tricks

- *The water and the sky will have the same undertone, but the water will be darker and grayer than the sky.*

- *Reflections follow the direction of the water flow and are NOT blended. Leave some of the blue water peeking out.*

- *Reflections distort and become less crisp as they move away from the object.*

Fruit

Yummy, crunchy, juicy! Each type has its own unique characteristics that make coloring them fun.

Materials
White smooth cardstock
Apples, Bananas and Oranges digital
    stamp
Markers: E29, E31, R22, R24, R39, YG63,
    YG67, Y11, Y17, YR04, YR09
Computer with printer

Apples

Whether they are red, yellow or green, apples contain a slick, shiny skin that needs stark highlights and deep shadows near the stem. Apples can be a variety of shades and can be a combination of reds and yellows or yellows and greens.

Make sure to leave the highlight white.

Step 1: Base the image with a light color (R22).

Don't forget the shadows around the stem.

Step 2: Add slight shadows by feathering in and blending a darker shade (R27).

Step 3: Feather in and blend the darkest shade (R39) to create deep shadows.

Bananas

They may seem difficult, but in reality they just require a few simple strokes.

Step 1: Base the image with a light color (Y11).

Make sure to follow the curve of the fruit.

Step 2: Add streaks of a darker shade (Y17) to the edges and bottom.

Step 3: Tone down shadows by streaking in a less saturated tone (E31). This will slightly blend any harsh lines.

Oranges

The unique orange peel texture is easy to replicate.

Step 1: Base the image with a light color (YR04). Leave an irregular white area for the highlight.

Step 2: Add dots of a darker color (YR09) for shading. Leave plenty of the light color visible.

Step 3: Dot in more of the darker color until the shadow half of the orange is dense and dark.

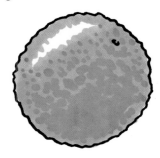

Sources: *White smooth X-Press It Blending Card and markers from Imagination International Inc.; digital stamp by Marianne Walker from included CD.*

Putting It All *Together*

Sometimes it can be intimidating to tackle an image with multiple objects. The following are some examples of how you can use the previous individual tutorials and simply apply them to more detailed images.

Here are some guidelines for tackling detailed images

- Always start with the most difficult area first. That way if you mess up, you won't have to redo the entire image.

- Break your images down into sections. Only focus on one section at a time, don't worry about the "whole."

- Remember, wet ink will blend easily. Always color in small sections.

The Fruit Bowl

The light source is coming from the front left in this example.

Materials
White smooth cardstock
Bowl of Fruit digital stamp
Markers: B24, B32, B34, B37, E29, E31, R22,
R27, R39, V12, V15, V17, Y11, Y17, YG23,
YG63, YG67, YR04, YR09
Computer with printer

Step 1: Start with the base of the image. Begin by coloring the bowl with B32 and adding B34 to the areas to be shaded.

Step 3: Base the pear with Y11 for a nice yellow glow. Add shading with YG23 and blend slightly. Color the grape leaves and vines with YG23 and YG67.

Step 5: Color the banana (following tutorial) with Y11, Y17 and E31.

Step 6: Color the orange (following tutorial) with YR04 and YR09. Remember to keep the white highlight irregular.

Remember to add a cast shadow from the rim.

Color grapes similar to the Flowers tutorial on page 18.

Step 7: Color the apple red (following tutorial) with R22, R27 and R39. Color the leaf with YG63, YG67 and the stem with E29.

Sources: White smooth X-Press It Blending Card and markers from Imagination International Inc.; digital stamp by Marianne Walker from included CD.

Step 2: Add B37 to shading on the bowl and gently blend together. Keep the shape of the bowl in mind and follow that shape with your strokes.

Step 4: Color the grapes with V12, V15 and V17. Begin by coloring and shading the whole bunch, and then add touches of shadows to each individual grape.

Feel free to add background and grounding to your image as desired.

The Wishing Well

The light source is coming from the upper right in this example.

Step 1: Begin by coloring the wooden roof with streaks of E31. In this case, we are going to treat the rope the same as the wood.

Step 4: Next, move on to the bricks and the stones. While they're two different areas, base them both with N1 for a neutral undertone.

Step 2: Add in steaks of E33; do not blend.

Step 5: Darken the shadows on the stones and the side of the well with irregular strokes of N3.

Remember to keep the shaded areas irregular.

Step 3: Complete the wooden structure by adding in shading with flicks of E47; do not blend.

Step 6: Add final rock shadows and darken random rocks in the well with N5.

Step 7: Color the entire footpath with E31. This goes over the neutral base and gives it a unified tone.

> *Color random bricks with E44 for contrast and interest.*

Step 8: Add the sky by flicking B00 from the image outward. Use the Colorless Blender to push the color back toward the image and soften edges.

Step 9: Add grass by basing with YG11 and then dabbing and dotting in YG67; do not blend.

Sources: White smooth X-Press It Blending Card, markers and Colorless Blender from Imagination International Inc.; digital stamp by Marianne Walker from included CD.

> *The flicks of grass will help cover any strong edges of the sky near the bottom.*

Materials

White smooth cardstock
Wishing Well digital stamp
Markers: B00, E31, E33, E44, E47, N1, N3, N5, YG11, YG67
Colorless Blender
Computer with printer

The Reflecting Pond

Typically you want to start with the hardest part of the image, but since the hardest part of this image is the reflection and that is added last, we will start with the rocks. The light source is coming from the upper right in this example.

Materials
White smooth cardstock
Koi Pond digital stamp
Markers: B00, B32, B34, E31, E43, G02, N1,
N3, N5, R22, YG63, YG67
Colorless Blender
Computer with printer

Step 1: Begin by coloring the rocks (following tutorial) with N1, N3 and N5.

Step 3: Add the foliage by coloring with a base of G02 and adding scribbles of YG63 and YG67. Color the cattails E31 and the lilies R22.

Step 2: Next, color the sky (following tutorial) with B00 and the Colorless Blender. Do not worry if part of the blue gets into the rocks or the uncolored grassy areas.

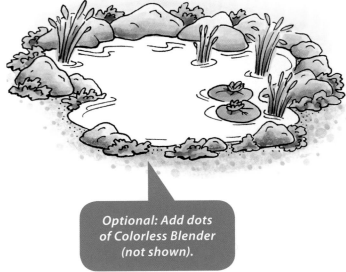

Optional: Add dots of Colorless Blender (not shown).

Step 4: Give the area some stability by grounding the front of the pond. Feather E43 and N3 from the base of the rocks out. Blend the edges with the Colorless Blender. Add dots of E43 and N3 in varying sizes.

Remember to leave some blue areas visible and do not blend the reflections.

Optional: Add a few streaks in the middle for ripples.

Step 5: Color the water with a color that is slightly darker and less saturated than the sky. Here the pond is based in B32. Make sure to leave white areas around the ripples for highlights.

Step 6: Darken the edges of the pond and around the foliage with B34.

Step 7: Finish the image by adding reflections. Add streaks of N3 and N5 to mirror the rocks, and add short streaks of YG67 to mirror the foliage.

Sources: *White smooth X-Press It Blending Card, markers and Colorless Blender from Imagination International Inc.; digital stamp by Marianne Walker from included CD.*

Keeping a *Record*

B000/B00/B01

B00/B01/B02

B00/B02/B06

B12/B14/B16

B12/B14/B18

B21/B24/B26

B32/B34/B37

B41/B45/B97

B60/B63/B66

B91/B93/B95

B91/B93/B95/B97

B00/B12/B24

Part of the learning process is recording and reflection. That's why we highly suggest you start your own Copic reference book.

Coloring Reference Book

Whether you call it a reference book, a swatch book, a color chart or a sketchbook, it's really just a place where you can collect and record information about Copic markers. This collection should become a well-used resource to help aid you on your Copic journey.

Tips and Tricks

- *Keep it organized. Separate colors into groups and keep separate areas for favorite techniques and practice images.*

- *Record sample color combinations. Start with natural blending groups and then start experimenting with alternative blending groups (as discussed in this book).*

- *Pick simple images that are not too large, yet have enough area to blend multiple colors.*

- *Write down everything—the paper, the ink, the name of the stamp and especially the colors used!*

- *Update it regularly. Make sure to start with a book large enough to add to over time.*

- *Review, reflect and explore! Flip through your book when you are in a rut or when you find yourself reaching for the same color groups.*

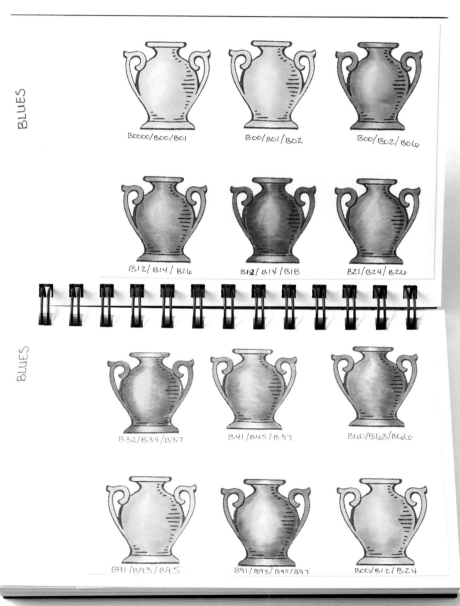

Stamp image from Layers of Color.

If you haven't started one yet, what are you waiting for? Do it now!

Going *Digital?*

In this book, we thought it would be a nice feature to include the original digital images that Marianne drew for the technique tutorials. We placed them on a disk that is included with the book so that you may print them off and practice the techniques along with us.

Tips and Tricks

- *Digital images typically are JPEG, TIFF or PNG files.*

- *Create a separate folder on the desktop and save images there.*

- *Fancy programs and equipment are not necessary for using digital images. Basic editing and printing can be done with MS Word or Adobe Photoshop and a printer.*

- *Test the printed images as you would a stamped image to make sure the paper/printer ink combination is compatible with Copic markers. If smearing occurs, you can heat-set the image or bring the printed images to an office supply store and photocopy them.*

Here's a Quick Lesson in Using Digi (using Microsoft Word®):

Since this is a book about Copic Coloring and not about digital stamping, we are only covering the very basics—enough to get you started using the images included on the disk.

Step 1. Save images to desktop folder.

Step 2. Open Word.

Step 3. In tool bar click Insert > Picture > From File.

Step 4. Select image and click Insert.

Step 5. In document, double click (or right click) image to bring up formatting box. Here you can format size, layout and lines.

Step 6. Once the image is ready, print as normal.

Avoid enlarging images over 100%. You'll notice bit mapping (jagged edges) in your image.

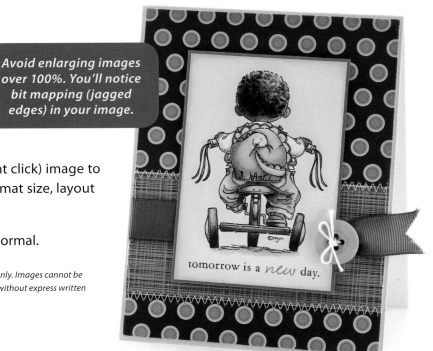

tomorrow is a *new* day.

All images are property of DRG Publishing and are for personal use only. Images cannot be reproduced in any way for sale, publication or educational purposes without express written permission from the publisher.

Creative Coloring *Projects*

Materials

Cardstock: white smooth, white, red
    Dotted Swiss, yellow Dotted Swiss
Green/white checkered printed paper
Stamps: Apple Background, "Thank You"
Black dye ink pad
Markers: BV01, BV04, E35, E40, E41, E42,
    E43, E44, E47, E79, R14, R24, R46, R59,
    Y02, Y11, YG01, YG03, YG13, YG23, YG63,
    YG67, YG95, YG99, YR04
Black multiliner (optional)
Colorless Blender refill (0)
Cloth
Adhesive foam tape
Double-sided adhesive

Apples

Design by **Jennifer Dove**

Techniques Used

- Blending Outside the Color Family
- Shadow & Shading Options
- How to Color … Fruit

Project note: *If "Thank You" stamp is unavailable, hand-print sentiment using multiliner.*

Coloring Instructions

1. Stamp image onto white smooth cardstock. Trim down to a 5 x 3⅞-inch panel with one leaf extending past edge of panel.

2. Color red apples with R14, R24, R46 and R59.

3. Color green apples with YG01, YG13, YG23 and YG95.

4. Color yellow apples with Y11, Y02, YR04 and BV01.

5. Color leaves with YG03, YG63, YG67 and YG99.

6. Color apple cores with E40, E41 and E42.

7. Color stems and background area with E35 and E79.

8. Dampen a cloth with Colorless Blender and press onto image to create texture.

9. Add dark cast shadows to any necessary area with BV04. Do not blend.

10. Stamp a second image onto a 5¼ x 2¼-inch piece of white smooth cardstock.

11. Color image with E40, E41, E42, E43, E44 and E47. In the same manner as before, add texture with cloth dampened with Colorless Blender.

12. Stamp or hand-print "Thank You" onto white smooth cardstock.

13. Cut a 2⅞ x1-inch rectangle around sentiment and color with E40, E42, E44 and E47. If desired, add texture in the same manner as before. ❧

Sources: *White cardstock from Neenah Paper; white smooth X-Press It Blending Card, markers, multiliner and Colorless Blender from Imagination International Inc.; Dotted Swiss cardstock from Bazzill Basics Paper Inc.; Apple Background stamp from The Peddler's Pack Stampworks; Memento ink pad from Tsukineko LLC; foam tape and double-sided adhesive from 3M.*

At Your Service

Design by **Colleen Schaan**

Techniques Used

- Blending Outside the Color Family
- How to Color … Metal

Coloring Instructions

1. Stamp image onto a 3 x 4-inch piece of white cardstock.

2. Color, blend and shade robot with C00, C1, C3 and C5. Leave highlights white and color in the direction of the shape.

3. Let dry completely. Add deep shading and cast shadows with C7. Do not blend.

4. Color face with C00. Add slight shading to the right side by feathering in C1. Color cheeks with C3.

5. Color chest and plastic on flowers with B000. Leave highlights white. Shade with B00 and blend gently.

6. Color heart and flowers with R21, R32, R37 and R89.

7. Color leaves with YG21, YG23 YG63 and G29. ❧

Sources: White smooth X-Press It Blending Card, markers, multiliner and double-sided tape from Imagination International Inc.; remaining cardstock from Bazzill Basics Paper Inc.; printed paper from Authentique Paper; stamp from Whiff of Joy; stamp set from My Favorite Things.

Materials

Cardstock: white smooth, black, blue
Journey Explore printed paper
Stamps: Beep Beep I Love You, Clearly Sentimental About You set
Black dye ink pad
Markers: B000, B00, C00, C1, C3, C5, C7, G29, R21, R32, R37, R89, YG21, YG23 YG63
Black multiliner
17 inches ⅝-inch-wide white ribbon
Craft wire
Heart charm
Craft knife
Double-sided tape

Bon Voyage

Design by Colleen Schaan

Techniques Used

- How to Color … Wood, Water, Sky

Coloring Instructions

1. Stamp images onto white cardstock.

2. Color sun with Y11, Y15 and Y17.

3. Add sky by flicking B0000 away from sun and blend edges with Colorless Blender.

4. Base water with B0000.

5. Add streaks of B41, B91, B32, B93 and B45. Do not blend.

6. Add reflection with streaks of Y15.

7. Color shadows on bird with W1 and B41.

8. Color beak with Y15.

9. Color wood with streaks of E53, E23, E57 and E79. Do not blend. ❧

Materials

Cardstock: white smooth, black, red Dotted Swiss
Stamp sets: Coastal Wishes, Fanciful Tags
Black dye ink pad
Markers: B0000, B32, B41, B45, B91, B93, E23, E53, E57, E79, W1, Y11, Y15, Y17
Colorless Blender (0)
Hemp twine
Classic Ovals SM die templates (#S4-112)
Die-cutting and embossing machine
Adhesive foam tape
Double-sided tape

Sources: *White smooth X-Press It Blending Card, markers, Colorless Blender, X-Press It foam tape and double-sided tape from Imagination International Inc.; remaining cardstock from Bazzill Basics Paper Inc.; Coastal Wishes stamp set from Our Craft Lounge; Fanciful Tags stamp set from Gina K. Designs; Memento ink pad from Tsukineko LLC; die templates from Spellbinders™ Paper Arts; die-cutting and embossing machine from Sizzix.*

Cheery Wishes

Design by **Lori Craig**

Techniques Used

- Blending Outside the Color Family
- How to Color … Flowers, Sky

Coloring Instructions

1. Stamp peonies image onto white cardstock with black ink.

2. Color and shade individual peony stems with R20, R32 and R43; do not blend.

3. Color roses with Y32, Y35 and Y38; do not blend.

4. Color stems with YG91, YG93 and YG95; do not blend. Use darkest color near base of stem.

5. Color planter with E31, E33, E35, E43, E44 and E47 using a series of flicks from top and bottom and leaving white space in center area for highlight. E47 will be used very sparingly, just under lip of container.

6. Use W0 and W1 to create a gentle illusion of a table for grounding of image.

7. Add sky with B000 and Colorless Blender. ❧

Sources: White smooth X-Press It Blending Card, markers, Colorless Blender, X-Press It foam tape and double-sided tape from Imagination International Inc.; printed paper from Echo Park Paper Co.; stamp set from Flourishes LLC; stamp from Lockhart Stamp Co.; Memento black dye ink pad from Tsukineko LLC; Mix'd Media Inx white pigment ink pad from Clearsnap Inc.; die from Taylored Expressions.

Materials

Cardstock: white smooth, kraft
Victoria Garden Garden Gate printed paper
Stamps: Spring Is Sprung set, Peonies
Ink pads: black dye, white pigment
Markers: B0000, E31, E33, E35, E43, E44, E47, R000, R01, R20, R32, R43, W0, W1, Y32, Y35, Y38, YG91, YG93, YG95
Colorless Blender (0)
Yellow buttons: 1 large, 2 small
Twine
Take Note Frame #3 die
Die-cutting machine
Sewing machine with white thread
Adhesive foam tape
Double-sided tape

SENDING
cheery
wishes
YOUR WAY

Dance in the Rain

Design by **Colleen Schaan**

Techniques Used

- Shadows & Shading Options
- How to Color … White, Black, Water

Coloring Instructions

1. Stamp image onto a 2⅞ x 3½-inch piece of white cardstock.

2. Color face with E21 and E33. Add E93 for cheeks and BV00 for cast shadow.

3. Base hair with B91. Add flicks of C3, C5 and C7. Do not blend.

4. Shade shirt and socks with C1.

5. Color shoes with C3, C5 and C7.

6. Color dress with Y11, Y17, YR16, YR09 and BV00.

7. Color puddle with BG0000 and B21. Blend edges with Colorless Blender.

8. Add reflections from shoes with C3.

9. Color white ribbon with B05; let dry. 🐾

Sources: White smooth X-Press It Blending Card, markers, Colorless Blender, multiliner, pigment paint, X-Press It foam tape and double-sided tape from Imagination International Inc.; Swiss Dot cardstock and Grandma's Feather Bed printed paper from Bazzill Basics Paper Inc.; Lauderdale printed papers from BasicGrey; stamp set from Kraftin' Kimmie Stamps; Memento ink pad from Tsukineko LLC; die from My Favorite Things.

Materials

Cardstock: white smooth, red Swiss Dot
Printed papers: Lauderdale Solar Flare, Lauderdale SPF, Grandma's Feather Bed Grandma's Damask
Dance in the Rain stamp set
Black dye ink pad
Markers: B05, B21, B91, BG0000, BV00, C1, C3, C5, C7, E21, E33, E93, Y11, Y17, YR09, YR16,
Colorless Blender (0)
Black multiliner
White pigment paint
3 inches ⅛-inch-wide white ribbon
White button
Open Scallop Edge die
Die-cutting machine
Paintbrush
Adhesive foam tape
Double-sided tape

Let Yourself Bloom

Design by **Colleen Schaan**

Techniques Used

- Blending Outside the Color Family
- How to Color … Foliage, Wood

Coloring Instructions

1. Stamp three trees and three wooden crates onto white smooth cardstock.

2. Color crates with flicks of E30, E34, E15 and E27. Do not blend.

3. Color trees with YG03, YG21 and G24.

4. Add loose scribbles of YG17, G17 and G28 to trees. Do not blend. 🐝

Materials

Cardstock: white smooth, lime green, light lime green, yellow
Picket Fence Cottage Garden printed paper
Stamp sets: DIY Topiary Trees, Hearts & Flowers
Black dye ink pad
Markers: E15, E27, E30, E34, G17, G24, G28, YG03, YG17, YG21
Black multiliner
Adhesive foam tape
Double-sided tape

Sources: White smooth X-Press It Blending Card, markers, multiliner, X-Press It foam tape and double-sided tape from Imagination International Inc.; remaining cardstock from Bazzill Basics Paper Inc.; printed paper from Lily Bee Design; stamp sets from Flourishes LLC; Memento ink pad from Tsukineko LLC.

F for Farm

Design by Marianne Walker

Techniques Used

- How to Color … Black, Ground, Metal, Sky

Coloring Instructions

1. Stamp image onto a 3¾ x 3-inch piece of white cardstock.

2. Color tractor with C1, C3 and C7. Cover whole tractor with YG63. Add highlights with Y11.

3. Color wheels with C1, N5 and N7.

4. Color ground with W3 and E31. Add dots of E31, C3, YG63 and Colorless Blender.

5. Add tractor shadow with C3.

6. Color grass with YG63, YG67 and G28.

7. Color sky with flicks of B41 and blend edges with Colorless Blender.

8. Color ribbon and chipboard letter "F" using YG67; let dry. ❧

Materials
Cardstock: white smooth, green, white
Green plaid printed paper
Chipboard letter "F"
Bountiful Harvest stamp set
Black dye ink pad
Markers: B41, C1, C3, C7, E31, G28, N5, N7, W3, Y11, YG11, YG63, YG67
Colorless Blender (0)
Multiliner
7 inches ¼-inch-wide white sheer ribbon
10 silver brads
Paper piercer
Double-sided tape

Sources: *White smooth X-Press It Blending Card, markers, Colorless Blender, multiliner and X-Press It double-sided tape from Imagination International Inc.; remaining cardstock from Neenah Paper and WorldWin Papers; stamp set from Our Craft Lounge; Memento ink pad from Tsukineko LLC.*

Miss You

Design by **Colleen Schaan**

Techniques Used
- How to Color … White, Black, Ground, Sky

Coloring Instructions

1. Stamp image onto a 3 x 3½-inch piece of white smooth cardstock.

2. Add shading to white areas with W00, W1 and W3 and blend edges with Colorless Blender.

3. Add cast shadows to white area with W5. Do not blend.

4. Color black stripes with C3, C5, C7 and C9.

5. Color nose and ears with R01, W1 and W3.

6. Color sky with B0000 and Colorless Blender.

7. Add ground with E30, E31 and E33. Blend edges with Colorless Blender.

8. Color ribbon using Black (100); let dry. ❧

Sources: *White smooth X-Press It Blending Card, markers, Colorless Blender, multiliner and X-Press It foam tape and double-sided tape from Imagination International Inc.; remaining cardstock from Bazzill Basics Paper Inc.; Honeymoon printed paper from Lily Bee Design; Al Fresco printed paper from Crate Paper Inc.; Zara stamp from Whipper Snapper Designs Inc.; Botanicals stamp set from Gina K. Designs; Memento ink pad from Tsukineko LLC; memo pin from Tim Holtz/Advantus Corp.; circle punches from Stampin' Up!*

Materials
Cardstock: white smooth, black, light brown
Printed papers: Portrait Honeymoon, Picket Fence Al Fresco
Stamps: Zara, Botanicals set
Black dye ink pad
Markers: B0000, Black (100), C3, C5, C7, C9, E30, E31, E33, R01, W00, W1, W3, W5
Colorless Blender (0)
Black multiliner
18 inches ⅝-inch-wide white grosgrain ribbon
2 black brads
Silver memo pin
Circle punches: 1⅜-inch, 1¼-inch
Sandwich bag
Paper piercer
Adhesive foam tape
Double-sided tape

It's Your Day

Design by Lori Craig

Techniques Used
• How to Color … Fur, Sky

Coloring Instructions

1. Stamp bear image onto white smooth cardstock. In the same manner, stamp image a second time, stamping only the sunflower.

2. Color bear image with E31, E33 and E35.

3. Add texture to bear by pouncing with Colorless Blender.

4. Color flower stem and blend with YG91, YG93 and YG95.

5. Color sky with BG0000 and Colorless Blender.

6. Color second stamped flower petals with flicks of Y32 and Y35.

7. Color second stamped flower center and blend with E43 and E44, leaving a light space toward center. ❧

Sources: *White cardstock from Neenah Paper; white smooth X-Press It Blending Card, markers, Colorless Blender, X-Press It foam tape and double-sided tape from Imagination International Inc.; remaining cardstock from Papertrey Ink; printed papers from Echo Park Paper Co.; stamp set from The Cat's Pajamas Rubber Stamps; Memento ink pad from Tsukineko LLC; die templates from Spellbinders™ Paper Arts.*

Materials
Cardstock: white smooth, kraft, dark brown
Dots & Stripes Candy Shoppe printed
    papers: Lemon Drops Small Dots,
    Chocolate Large Dot
Bearing Flowers stamp set
Brown dye ink pad
Markers: BG0000, E31, E33, E35, E43, E44,
    Y32, Y35, YG91, YG93, YG95
Colorless Blender (0)
7⅝ inches ¼-inch-wide white ruffled
    ribbon
Twine
Die templates: Floral Doily Motifs (#S5-041),
    Standard Circles LG (#S4-114)
Die-cutting machine
Sewing machine with white thread
Adhesive foam tape
Double-sided tape

Tomorrow Is a New Day

Design by **Debbie Olson**

Techniques Used
- Blending Outside the Color Family
- How to Color … White, Black, Sky

Coloring Instructions

1. Print digital image onto white smooth cardstock; trim to 2½ x 3⅝ inches.

2. Color jeans with B91, B95, B97, BV00 and BV02.

3. Color backpack with YG11, YG13, YG17 and BV02. Color with glitter pens as desired.

4. Using tiny dots, color hair with N1, N3 and N7.

5. Color skin with E13 and E15.

6. Color tricycle with R32 and R37.

7. Color wheels and seat with N1, N3 and N7.

8. Color sky with B0000 and Colorless Blender. Color edges of image panel using E13. ❧

Sources: White smooth X-Press It Blending Card, markers, Colorless Blender, glitter pens, X-Press It foam tape and double-sided tape from Imagination International Inc.; remaining cardstock and stamp set from Papertrey Ink; digital stamp from Mo's Digital Pencil; Memento ink pads from Tsukineko LLC.

Materials
Cardstock: white smooth, white, green
Printed papers: green dots, green stripes
Stamps: Bye Bye Boy digital, Blooming Button Bits set
Dye ink pads: black, green
Markers: B0000, B91, B95, B97, BV00, BV02, E13, E15, N1, N3, N7, R32, R37, YG11, YG13, YG17
Colorless Blender (0)
Glitter pens: clear, green
Green button
6½ inches ⅝-inch-wide white ribbon
White crochet thread
Sewing machine with white thread
Adhesive foam tape
Double-sided tape
Computer with printer

Sending Hugs

Design by **Michelle Houghton**

Techniques Used

- Blending Outside the Color Family
- Shadow & Shading Options
- How to Color … Foliage

Coloring Instructions

1. Print image twice onto white smooth cardstock.

2. Color base of treetop with YG0000. Add squiggles with YG93, YG95, YG97 and BG99. Do not blend. **Note:** *In the same manner, color edges of second treetop image.*

3. Dampen a cloth with Colorless Blender and dab treetop.

4. Working on second printed image, color tree trunk with flicks of YR31, E33, E25 and E09.

5. Color sweater and leggings with YR30 and YR31.

6. Color dress with B60, B63 and B66.

7. Fill shoes and headband with B66.

8. Color skin with YR000, YR01 and BV00.

9. Add cheeks with R22.

10. Color hair with flicks of Y23, Y26, E33 and E29.

11. Color grass with flicks of YG93 and YG97.

12. Add shadows on tree trunk with BV04. ✎❧

Sources: White smooth X-Press It Blending Card and Colorless Blender refill from Imagination International Inc.; Sweet Threads printed papers from BasicGrey; Lime Twist printed paper from My Mind's Eye; digital stamp from Tiddly Inks; foam dots and double-sided adhesive from 3M.

Materials

White smooth cardstock
Printed papers: Sweet Threads I Need, Sweet Threads Fashionista, Lime Twist Fly A Kite Soar Fly die cut
Tree Hugger digital stamp
Markers: BV00, BV04, B60, B63, B66, BG99, E09, E25, E29, E33, R22, Y23, Y26, YG0000, YG93, YG95, YG97, YR000, YR01, YR30, YR31
Colorless Blender refill (0)
Brown twine
Yellow button
Cloth
Adhesive dot
Adhesive foam dots
Double-sided adhesive
Computer with printer

Perfect Pears

Design by Sharon Harnist

Techniques Used

- Blending Outside the Color Family
- Shadow & Shading Options
- How to Color … Fruit

Coloring Instructions

1. Stamp image onto white smooth cardstock.

2. Base most of pears with YG0000, adding YR0000 in one spot on each pear for variation.

3. Add shading to green areas with YG01, YG03 and YG63.

4. Add shading to orange areas with YR01.

5. Add dots of E31 and E35 to deepen shadows.

6. Add dots of Colorless Blender to pears to create texture.

7. Color and shade leaf with YG03, YG63 and stems with E31 and E35.

8. Ground pears with W00 and W2. 🐞

Sources: White smooth X-Press It Blending Card, markers, Colorless Blender, X-Press It foam tape and double-sided tape from Imagination International Inc.; remaining cardstock from Gina K. Designs and Memory Box; Perfect Pears stamp from Lockhart Stamp Co.; stamp set from Gina K. Designs; Memento ink pad from Tsukineko LLC; punch from Stampin' Up!; die templates and embossing folder from Spellbinders™ Paper Arts.

Sending you SUNSHINE

Sending You Sunshine

Design by **Debbie Olson**

Techniques Used

- Blending Outside the Color Family
- How to Color … Fruit

Coloring Instructions

1. Stamp image onto a 2¼ x 3½-inch piece of white cardstock with black ink.

2. Color strawberries with R20, R22, R35, R39 and R59.

3. Color leaves with YG00, YG01, YG13 and YG17.

4. Color background on left with G000 and on right with B000. Add shadows underneath strawberries and on lower left with BV000.

5. Stamp jar top on white cardstock and color with T1 and T3. Trim closely.

6. Stamp jar ruffle onto Pleated Skirt Glittered paper; trim closely and shade with T1.

7. Place seam binding in a sandwich bag and add several drops of R20 and R27 ink refills. Squeeze bag to ink seam binding thoroughly. Remove from bag; let dry. ❧

Sources: *White smooth X-Press It Blending Card, markers, ink refills, glitter pen, X-Press It foam tape and double-sided tape from Imagination International Inc.; remaining cardstock and stamp sets from Papertrey Ink; printed papers from My Mind's Eye; die templates from Spellbinders™ Paper Arts.*

Materials

Cardstock: white smooth, cream, pink
Lost and Found Market Street printed
   papers: Princess, Princess Crowns
   Glittered, Love Demure, Adore Pleated
   Skirt Glittered
Stamp sets: Friendship Jar, Friendship Jar
   Summer Fillers, Simple Sunflower
Dye ink pads: black, red, light brown
Markers: B000, BV000, G000, R20, R22, R35,
   R39, R59, T1, T3, YG00, YG01, YG13, YG17
Ink refills: R20, R27
Clear glitter pen
15 inches ½-inch-wide white seam binding
Cream crochet thread
4 white buttons
Die templates: Classic Scallop (#E8-001),
   Nested Lacey Pennants (#S5-029)
Die-cutting and embossing machine
Sanding block
Sandwich bag
Sewing machine with white thread
Adhesive foam tape
Double-sided adhesive

Sunny the Turtle

Design by **Melanie Holtz**

Techniques Used

- Blending Outside the Color Family
- Shadow & Shading Options
- How to Color … Water

Project note: Ink edges of cut pieces using brown distress ink as desired.

Coloring Instructions

1. Stamp image onto a 4⅛ x 3-inch piece of white smooth cardstock.

2. Color turtle with YG00, YG03, YG67 and G99.

3. Add dots of YG67, G99 and C5 to create texture.

4. Color shell with E50, E11, E13, E25, E29 and E49.

5. Color duck with Y11, Y17, YR04 and YR07.

6. Color bottle with BG72 and BG75.

7. Color water with B00, B02, B05, BG0000, BG000 and BG10. Leave some areas white.

8. Add reflections with YG03, Y00, E50, E11 and E13.

9. Create a sky by masking image with a cloud template and using a cosmetic wedge to sponge blue distress ink over template. ***Note:*** *Hand-trim a piece of scrap cardstock to make cloud template. Move template as desired to create more clouds while inking.*

10. If desired, apply clear dimensional gloss medium to water surface; do not apply to duck. Let dry. ❧

Sources: White smooth cardstock from Neenah Paper; remaining cardstock from Bazzill Basics Paper Inc.; printed papers from Fancy Pants Designs; stamp from Kraftin' Kimmie Stamps; Memento black ink pad from Tsukineko LLC; distress ink pads and clear dimensional gloss medium from Ranger Industries Inc.; markers from Imagination International Inc.; paper adhesive from Tombow USA.

Materials

Cardstock: white smooth, kraft, dark brown, green
Happy Together printed papers: Makes Me Smile, You and Me
Sunny The Turtle stamp
Dye ink pads: black, brown distress, blue distress
Markers: B00, B02, B05, BG0000, BG000, BG10, BG72, BG75, C3, C5, C7, E08, E11, E13, E25, E29, E33, E49, E50, G99, Y00, Y11, Y17, YG00, YG03, YG67, YR04, YR07
Cosmetic wedge
Sewing machine with cream thread
Clear dimensional gloss medium
Paper adhesive

Swan Lake

Design by **Colleen Schaan**

Techniques Used
- Blending Outside the Color Family
- How to Color ... White, Flowers, Sky, Water

Project note: *Masking was used in creating the swan/lake scenes.*

Coloring Instructions

1. Stamp images twice onto white cardstock. ***Note:*** *Referring to photo, only color edges of second stamped image.*

2. Add shading to swan with touches of C00 and C1.

3. Color swan's bill with YR65.

4. Color reflected swan with C00.

5. Color water with B0000, B000 and C00.

6. Add touches of C1 to reflected swan and B91 to edges of water and ripples.

7. Color sky with B91 and Colorless Blender.

8. Color grasses with flicks of YG25, G24 and G29. Do not blend.

9. Color ground with E31.

10. Color flowers with BV000, BV00, BV11 and BV17; dot V04 into centers.

11. Add grass reflections with short streaks of G21.

Sources: *White smooth X-Press It Blending Card, markers, Colorless Blender, X-Press It foam tape and double-sided tape from Imagination International Inc.; remaining cardstock from Bazzill Basics Paper Inc.; stamp set from Flourishes LLC; Cuttlebug embossing folder from Provo Craft; die templates from Spellbinders™ Paper Arts; die-cutting and embossing machine from Sizzix.*

Materials
Cardstock: white smooth, light blue, lavender
Masking material
Swan Lake set
Black dye ink pad
Markers: B0000, B000, B91, BV000, BV00, BV11, BV17, C00, C1, E31, G21, G24, G29, V04, YG25, YR65
Colorless Blender (0)
20 inches ⅝-inch-wide white satin ribbon
Purple fabric flowers
4 white pearl brads
Textile Texture embossing folder (#37-1153)
Die templates: Labels One (#S4-161), Standard Circles SM (#S4-116), Standard Circles LG (#S4-114)
Die-cutting and embossing machine
Paper piercer
Repositionable adhesive
Adhesive foam tape
Double-sided tape

United We Stand

Design by **Colleen Schaan**

Techniques Used

- Blending Outside the Color Family
- Shadow & Shading Options
- How to Color … Ground, Sky

Project note: *Ink edges light brown as desired.*

Coloring Instructions

1. Stamp image onto a 2⅝ x 3¾-inch piece of white cardstock with black ink.

2. Color skin with E50, E21 and E31.

3. Color clothing with E81, YG91, YG93, YG95 and E87.

4. Color spots with E81, E42, E23, E57 and E29.

5. Color with E21, E23, E57 and E29.

6. Color glasses with W1, W3, W5 and W7.

7. Color sky with B0000 and Colorless Blender.

8. Add ground by layering E50, E41, E11, E43 and E23, blending edges slightly. Add dots of E17 and E87.

9. Add cast shadow under shoes with E87.

10. Add extra shading and cast shadows to entire image with W5.

11. Add highlights to image using white pigment paint; let dry. ❧

Sources: *White smooth X-Press It Blending Card, markers, Colorless Blender, pigment paint, multiliner, X-Press It foam tape and double-sided tape from Imagination International Inc.; remaining cardstock from Bazzill Basics Paper Inc.; printed paper from SEI; Military Boy stamp from Whipper Snapper Designs Inc.; United We Stand stamp from PrintWorks Collection Inc.; Memento ink pad from Tsukineko LLC; distress ink pad from Ranger Industries Inc.; die templates from Spellbinders™ Paper Arts.*

THANKS a Bunch

Design by **Claudia Rosa**

Techniques Used

- How to Color … White, Black, Wood, Metal, Sky

Project note: *Distress edges of cut pieces using sandpaper and ink edges light brown using blending tool as desired. If "THANKS A BUNCH" stamp is unavailable, use rub-on transfers or hand-print sentiment.*

Coloring Instructions

1. Stamp image onto a 3¾ x 4½-inch piece of white cardstock with black ink.

2. Stamp image onto masking material; cut out to create a mask.

3. Place masking image on top of main image and stamp basket of apples. Remove mask.

4. Color skin with E0000, E00 and E13. Add cheeks with R20.

5. Color overalls with E70, E71, E74 and E79.

6. Color shoes with W00, W1, W2, W3, W4, W5 and W7.

7. Color shirt with C00, C0, C3, C4, C5 and C6.

8. Color apples, hairband and grass with Y000, Y00, YG25, YG93, YG95 and YG99.

9. Color hair with flicks of E50, E31, E13, E27 and E37.

10. Color basket with E00, E31 and E13.

11. Color trim and shovel with C00, C0, C3, C4 and C5.

12. Create background by adding dots of W00, W1, W2, W3, W4, W5 and W7. Do not blend. ✑

Sources: *White smooth X-Press It Blending Card, markers, Colorless Blender, X-Press It foam tape and double-sided tape from Imagination International Inc.; remaining cardstock, brads and flat-back pearls from Michaels Stores Inc.; Garden Tilda stamp, Apples Basket stamp and #3 Tilda Lace die from MAGNOLIA-licious; Memento ink pad from Tsukineko LLC; distress ink pad from Ranger Industries Inc.; Cuttlebug Vintage Die set from Provo Craft; remaining die templates from Spellbinders™ Paper Arts; quick-drying paper adhesive from 3M.*

Materials

Cardstock: white smooth, dark brown, light brown, kraft
Printed papers: checkered apples, green checkered, green damask
White paper doily
Masking material
Stamps: Garden Tilda, Apple Basket, "THANKS A BUNCH"
Dye ink pads: black, brown distress
Markers: C00, C0, C3, C4, C5, C6, E0000, E00, E13, E27, E31, E37, E50, E70, E71, E74, E79, R20, W00, W0, W1, W2, W3, W4, W5, W7, Y000, Y00, YG25, YG93, YG95, YG99
17 inches ³⁄₁₆-inch-wide brown/white ribbon
8 inches 1-inch-wide cream lace
Natural twine
Green silver backed flat-back pearls: 1 extra large, 1 medium, 2 small
Copper spiral clip
Copper ribbon buckle
Die templates: #3 Tilda Lace, Cuttlebug Vintage Die set (#37-1202), Standard Circles SM (#S4-116), Petite Scalloped Circles SM (#S4-117)
Die-cutting machine
Blending tool
Sandpaper
Sewing machine with white thread
Quick-drying paper adhesive

Materials

Cardstock: white smooth, bright pink, kraft
Victoria Gardens Rose printed paper
Berry Sweet stamp
Ink pads: black dye, white pigment
Markers: BG0000, G21, G24, G28, R00, R37, R59, RV21, RV23, RV25, YG00, YG03, YG06
Colorless Blender (0)
White paper flowers
Red buttons: 3 small, 1 medium
Natural twine
6 inches ⅝-inch-wide white lace
Dots and Flowers embossing folder set (#655838)
Take Note Frame #3 die
Die-cutting and embossing machine
Craft sponge
Adhesive foam tape
Double-sided tape

So Sweet

Design by Lori Craig

Techniques Used
- Blending Outside the Color Family
- How to Color … White, Foliage

Coloring Instructions

1. Using black ink, stamp raspberry image onto white smooth cardstock. Repeat, only stamping two small blossoms from top of raspberry image.

2. Color berries with RV21, RV23 and RV25, leaving white space on varying portions of each berry.

3. Shade berries with R37 and R59.

4. Add highlights to berries with YG00.

5. Using R00, color both smaller blossoms at top of image. Color center of blossoms with YG00. Repeat to color second set of blossom images.

6. Color leaves with YG00, YG03, YG06, G21, G24 and G28.

7. Color sky with BG0000 and Colorless Blender. ✤

Sources: White smooth X-Press It Blending Card, markers, Colorless Blender, X-Press It foam tape and double-sided tape from Imagination International Inc.; remaining cardstock from Bazzill Basics Paper Inc. and Papertrey Ink; printed paper from Echo Park Paper Co.; stamp from Flourishes LLC; Memento black dye ink pad from Tsukineko LLC; Mix'd Media Inx white pigment ink pad from Clearsnap Inc.; paper flower from Prima Marketing Inc.; embossing folder set from Sizzix; die from Taylored Expressions.

Sunshine & Love

Design by **Colleen Schaan**

Techniques Used

- How to Color … Foliage, Coloring Rocks, Wood, Sky

Coloring Instructions

1. Print image onto white cardstock and trim to approximately 3½ x 4¾ inches, allowing some images to extend past edges of panel.

2. Color rocks with W00, W1, W3, W5 and W7. Do not blend. Add dots of varying sizes of C7, C5, C3 and C1 to add slight texture.

3. Color tree trunk with E21, E57 and E79. Leave colors streaky.

4. Color base of leaves on tree with G00 and YG03. Add scribbles with G05, G16 and G28. Do not blend.

5. Color base of grass with YG21. Add scribbles with YG13, G02, G14, G16 and G07. Do not blend.

6. Color base of flower leaves with G40. Add shading with YG41, G28 and YG67.

7. Color flowers with RV66 or Y11 and Y06.

8. Color butterflies with RV63 and BV00.

9. Color birds with R11, E23 and E15.

10. Add flicks of B41 to bottom of each cloud and blend to white with Colorless Blender.

11. Color sky with B0000 and Colorless Blender. ✍

Sources: *White smooth X-Press It Blending Card, markers, Colorless Blender, X-Press It foam tape and double-sided tape from Imagination International Inc.; remaining cardstock from Bazzill Basics Paper Inc.; digital stamp from Make It Crafty; stamp set from JustRite; Memento ink pad from Tsukineko LLC; die templates from Spellbinders™ Paper Arts; die-cutting machine from Sizzix.*

Materials

Cardstock: white smooth, blue, light blue
Stamps: Timber Top Ridge digital, love sentiment
Black dye ink pad
Markers: B0000, B41, BV00, C1, C3, C5, C7, E15, E21, E23, E57, E79, G00, G02, G05, G07, G14, G16, G28, G40, R11, RV63, RV66, W00, W1, W3, W5, W7, Y06, Y11, YG03, YG13, YG21, YG41, YG67
Colorless Blender (0)
2 inches ⅜-inch-wide lime green/white dot ribbon
Die templates: Standard Circles SM (#S4-116), Standard Circles LG (#S4-1140)
Die-cutting machine
Adhesive foam tape
Double-sided tape

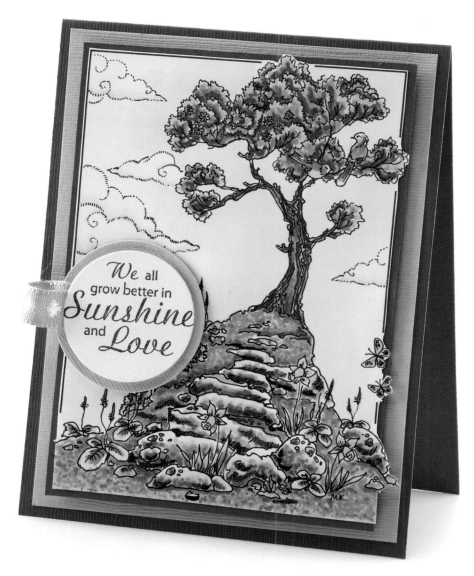

We all grow better in *Sunshine* and *Love*

Just Married

Design by **Colleen Schaan**

Techniques Used

- Blending Outside the Color Family
- How to Color … Black, Fur

Coloring Instructions

1. Stamp image onto a 3⅞ x 5⅛-inch piece of white smooth cardstock.

2. Color male bunny's fur with E41, E43, E44 and E47.

3. Color cheeks and ears with E40, E21 and E93.

4. Color girl bunny's fur with E000, E00, E13 and E25.

5. Color cheeks and ears with R11 and R81.

6. Dampen a cloth with Colorless Blender refill and place over colored image to create fur texture.

7. Color jacket and top hat with C1, C3, C5 and C7.

8. Add Y35 and Y28 to the buttons.

9. Color bonnet with RV00, R81 and RV34.

10. Color hat bands and bow with R81, RV34, RV66 and RV99.

11. Shade envelope with C1.

12. Add ground with E11 and E13, and feather to white with Colorless Blender.

12. Referring to photo, color ribbon using R81 and RV34. In the same manner, color a small piece of cotton thread. ❧

Sources: White smooth X-Press It Blending Card, markers, Colorless Blender, multiliner, X-Press It foam tape and double-sided tape from Imagination International Inc.; remaining cardstock from Bazzill Basics Paper Inc.; printed paper from My Mind's Eye; stamp from Stampavie; stamp set from Verve Stamps; Memento ink pad from Tsukineko LLC; Wedding Charms from Making Memories.

Materials

Cardstock: white smooth, mauve, pink, black
Lime Twist Happy Go Lucky Cute Blossoms Die-Cut printed paper
Stamps: Vintage Bunnies, Text Object set
Black dye ink pad
Markers: C1, C3, C5, C7, E000, E00, E11, E13, E21, E25, E40, E41, E43, E44, E47, E93, R11, R81, RV00, RV34, RV66, RV99, Y28, Y35
Colorless Blender (0)
Colorless Blender refill
White cotton thread
16 inches ⅝-inch-wide white satin ribbon
Wedding Charms: Just Married
Soft cloth
Adhesive foam tape
Double-sided tape

Always Have High Hopes

Materials

Cardstock: white smooth, black
Journey Explore printed paper
Stamps: Joy digital, Up, Up and Away set
Black dye ink pad
Markers: B05, B24, BV00, C00, E00, E33, E93,
   N0, N2, N4, N6, N8
Multiliners: yellow, black
3½ inches ⅝-inch-wide white satin ribbon
Black cord
White button
Adhesive foam tape
Double-sided tape
Computer with printer

High Hopes

Design by **Colleen Schaan**

Techniques Used

• How to Color … White, Black

Coloring Instructions

1. Print image onto white cardstock and trim to 3¼ x 3½ inches.

2. Color skin with E00 and E33. Add E93 for cheeks and BV00 for cast shadows.

3. Color robes with N0, N2, N4, N6 and N8.

4. Shade collars with C00.

5. Color chains and crosses with a yellow multiliner.

6. Color ribbon using B05 and B24. ❧

Sources: White smooth X-Press It Blending Card, markers, multiliners, X-Press It foam tape and double-sided tape from Imagination International Inc.; remaining cardstock from Bazzill Basics Paper Inc.; printed paper from Authentique Paper; digital stamp from Mo's Digital Pencil; stamp set from My Favorite Things; Memento ink pad from Tsukineko LLC; self-adhesive rhinestones from Kaisercraft.

Let Freedom Ring

Design by **Claudia Rosa**

Techniques Used

- Blending Outside the Color Family
- How to Color … White, Sky

Coloring Instructions

1. Stamp image onto a 4½ x 5-inch piece of white smooth cardstock with black ink.

2. Stamp image onto scrap paper and cut out to create a mask.

3. Attach mask over main image using repositionable tape and stamp starburst image onto image panel as shown. Remove mask.

4. Use multiliner to draw stripes onto flag.

5. Color skin with E0000, E00 and E13. Add cheeks with R20.

6. Color dress and stripes with B60, B63, B66 and B69. Color stars on dress with glitter pen.

7. Color shoes and stripes with R000, R21, R24 and R46.

8. Color hair by adding flicks of E50, E31, E27 and E37. Do not blend.

9. Color stars with Y00, Y18, Y35 and Y38.

10. Add background with dots of W00, W1, W2, W3 and Colorless Blender.

11. Add ground with W00, W1, W3 and E31. ❧

Sources: White smooth X-Press It Blending Card, markers, Colorless Blender, glitter pen, X-Press It foam tape and double-sided tape from Imagination International Inc.; remaining cardstock from Bazzill Basics Paper Inc.; Tilda in Star Dress stamp, Shooting Stars stamp and die from MAGNOLIA-licious; Memento black dye ink pad from Tsukineko LLC; distress ink pad from Ranger Industries Inc.; quick-drying paper adhesive from 3M; tacky glue from iLoveToCreate™.

Materials

Cardstock: white smooth, white pearlescent, kraft, dark blue
Printed papers: blue/white star, red/white stripe
Scrap paper
Stamps: Tilda in Star Dress, Shooting Stars, patriotic- and birthday-themed sentiments, 2-inch circle
Dye ink pads: black, brown distress
Markers: B60, B63, B66, B69, E0000, E00, E13, E27, E31, E37, E50, R000, R20, R21, R24, R46, W00, W1, W2, W3, Y00, Y18, Y35, Y38
Colorless Blender (0)
Iridescent glitter pen
22 inches ¼-inch-wide blue ribbon
8 inches 1½-inch-wide white lace
Twine
Red button
7 clear self-adhesive gems
White self-adhesive pearl
4 silver brads
Antique Lace die
Die-cutting machine
Paper piercer
Craft knife
Craft sponge
Sewing machine with white thread
Repositionable tape
Quick-drying paper adhesive
Tacky glue

HAPPY
BIRTHDAY
TO: **america**
let freedom ring
№ ....
AND MANY MORE

Let's Fly Away

Design by **Tammy Hershberger**

Techniques Used

- Blending Outside the Color Family
- How to Color … White

Coloring Instructions

1. Stamp image onto a 4 x 4-inch piece of white smooth cardstock.

2. Color body of plane with R12, R14, R17 and R29.

3. Color wing and trim with BG11, BG13 and BG49.

4. Color propeller and exhaust pipe with T1, T3 and T5.

5. Color aviator cap with E21, E23 and E25.

6. Color goggles with T3 and T5.

7. Color nose with R30, R32 and R35.

8. Shade exhaust with C1 and C2 and blend edges with Colorless Blender.

9. Shade rabbit with C00, C0, C1 and C2 and blend edges with Colorless Blender. ❧

Sources: White smooth X-Press It Blending Card, markers, Colorless Blender and multiliner from Imagination International Inc.; remaining cardstock and foam dots from Stampin' Up!; printed papers from October Afternoon; stamp set from The Cat's Pajamas Rubber Stamps; Memento ink pad from Tsukineko LLC; Rainbows & Clouds die set from Lil' Inker Designs; Simply Scallops die from My Favorite Things; Glossy Accents from Ranger Industries Inc.; paper adhesive from Tombow USA.

Materials

Cardstock: white smooth, red, blue, kraft
Printed papers: The Thrift Shop Great Find, Seaside Swim Trunks, Seaside Yellow Bikini
Take Off stamp set
Black dye ink pad
Markers: BG11, BG13, BG49, C00, C0, C1, C2, E21, E23, E25, R12, R14, R17, R29, R30, R32, R35, T1, T3, T5
Colorless Blender (0)
19 inches ⅝-inch-wide aqua ribbon
Blue button
3 red round brads
Red/white baker's twine
Dies: Rainbows & Clouds set, Simply Scallops, tag
Die-cutting and embossing machine
Paper piercer
Sandwich bag
Clear dimensional gloss medium
Adhesive foam dots
Paper adhesive

You Rock

Design by **Colleen Schaan**

Techniques Used

- Blending Outside the Color Family
- Shadow & Shading Options
- How to Color … Rocks, Ground, Sky

Coloring Instructions

1. Print images onto white smooth cardstock.

2. Using a multiliner, draw in top of cave and trim to a 4 x 2¾-inch piece.

3. Base cave and rocks with W00.

4. Add dots of varying sizes of W1, W3, W5, W7, C7, C5, C3 and C1 to create shading and texture.

5. Color sky with B41 and Colorless Blender.

6. Ground image with E41, E42, E43, E44 and E55.

7. Color skin with E21 and E34.

8. Add cheeks with R02 and cast shadow with BV01.

9. Color hair by flicking with YR30, YR21, YR24, YR14 and E99. Do not blend.

10. Color dress with Y21, YR24 and YR14. ❧

Sources: White smooth X-Press It Blending Card, markers, Colorless Blender, multiliner, X-Press It foam tape and double-sided tape from Imagination International Inc.; remaining cardstock from Bazzill Basics Paper Inc.; digital stamps from Tiddly Inks; stamp set from Gina K. Designs; Memento ink pad from Tsukineko LLC.

Materials

Cardstock: white smooth, black, tan
Stamps: Ugga Bugga Dive digital, Cave digital, Live Life Loud set
Black dye ink pad
Markers: B41, BV01, C1, C3, C5, C7, E21, E34, E41, E42, E43, E44, E55, E99, R02, W00, W1, W3, W5, W7, Y21, YR14, YR21, YR24, YR30
Colorless Blender (0)
Black multiliner
5 black brads
Paper piercer
Adhesive foam tape
Double-sided tape
Computer with printer

Materials

Cardstock: white smooth, maroon
Lime Twist Happy Go Lucky printed papers:
 Cute Buttons, Perfect Lines, Happy
 Blooms
Stamps: Clarabelle, Fairy Sentiments set
Black dye ink pad
Markers: BG0000, BG10, BG13, C00, C1, C3,
 E000, E00, E11, E31, E33, E35, E57, R20,
 R81, R83, R85, R89, Y0000, YG03, YG05,
 YG93
Colorless Blender (0)
R59 ink refill
Charm Pin Up Brad
6 inches ½-inch-wide white seam binding
Sandwich bag
Paper piercer
Paper adhesive

You're Enchanting

Design by Michele Boyer

Techniques Used

- Shadow & Shading Options
- How to Color … Sky

Coloring Instructions

1. Stamp image onto a 2⅞ x 3¾-inch piece of white smooth cardstock.

2. Color skin with E000, E00 and E11.

3. Add cheeks with R20.

4. Color hair with flicks of E31, E33, E35 and E57.

5. Outline left edges of eyes with BG0000.

6. Color leotard with R81, R83, R85 and R89.

7. Color stripes on arms and legs using YG93, YG03, R81 and BG13. Add shading with C3.

8. Color wings with BG0000, BG10 and BG13.

9. Flick in grass with YG03 and YG05. Add shadow at grass base using C00 and C1.

10. Color sky with Y0000 and Colorless Blender.

11. Place seam binding in a sandwich bag and add several drops of R59 ink refill. Squeeze bag to ink seam binding thoroughly. Remove from bag; let dry. ❧

Sources: White smooth X-Press It Blending Card, markers, Colorless Blender and ink refill from Imagination International Inc.; maroon cardstock from Bazzill Basics paper Inc.; printed papers from My Mind's Eye; stamps from Kraftin' Kimmie Stamps; Memento ink pad from Tsukineko LLC; Charm Pin Up Brad from Karen Foster Design.

Contributors

Michele Boyer
http://papercuts.blogs.splitcoaststampers.com/
You're Enchanting, 62

Lori Craig
http://loricraig.blogs.splitcoaststampers.com/
Cheery Wishes, 37
It's Your Day, 42
So Sweet, 54

Jennifer Dove
http://just4funcrafts.blogspot.com/
Apples, 34

Sharon Harnist
http://paperfections.typepad.com
Perfect Pears, 45

Tammy Hershberger
http://stamphappy-tammy.blogspot.com/
Let's Fly Away, 60

Melanie Holtz
http://paperblessingsbymelanie.blogspot.com/
Sunny the Turtle, 49

Michelle Houghton
http://www.scrapweaver.com/
Sending Hugs, 44

Debbie Olson
http://debbiedesigns.typepad.com
Tomorrow Is a New Day, 43
Sending You Sunshine, 47

Claudia Rosa
http://rosaswelt.blogspot.com/
THANKS a Bunch, 53
Let Freedom Ring, 58

Colleen Schaan
www.distinctivetouches.com
At Your Service, 35
Bon Voyage, 36
Dance in the Rain, 38

Let Yourself Bloom, 39
Miss You, 41
Swan Lake, 50
United We Stand, 51
Sunshine & Love, 55
Just Married, 56
High Hopes, 57
You Rock, 61

Marianne Walker
http://ilikemarkers.blogspot.com/
F for Farm, 40

About the Authors

Colleen Schaan is a Regional Copic Certification Instructor and team member of the Fine Art Education program in North America and travels extensively across the nation for workshops, demos and trade shows. She holds English and secondary education degrees from Wartburg College and taught English at the middle school, high school and college levels for 12 years before retiring to focus on a career in creative arts. She currently resides in Atlanta, Ga., with her husband and three pets.

Marianne Walker is the Product Director for Imagination International Inc., where she develops product publications and certification manuals. She is the Lead Illustrator for Our Craft Lounge and the author of *Shadows & Shading: A Beginner's Guide to Lighting Placement*. She travels throughout the United States teaching drawing and coloring classes at trade shows, stores and art schools. She graduated from the University of Oregon with a bachelor of fine arts in multimedia design and a minor in journalism/advertising. She currently resides in Springfield, Ore., with her husband and two children.

Buyer's Guide

3M
(800) 328-6276
www.scotchbrand.com

Authentique Paper
(800) 374-8070
www.authentiquepaper.com

BasicGrey
(801) 544-1116
www.basicgrey.com

Bazzill Basics Paper Inc.
(800) 560-1610
www.bazzillbasics.com

The Cat's Pajamas Rubber Stamps
www.thecatspajamasrs.com

Clearsnap Inc.
(800) 448-4862
www.clearsnap.com

Cosmo Cricket
(800) 852-8810
www.cosmocricket.com

The Crafter's Workshop
(877) 272-3837
www.thecraftersworkshop.com

Crate Paper Inc.
(801) 798-8996
www.cratepaper.com

Echo Park Paper Co.
(800) 701-1115
www.echoparkpaper.com

Fancy Pants Designs
(801) 779-3212
www.fancypantsdesigns.com

Flourishes LLC
(888) 475-1575
http://flourishes.org

Gina K. Designs
(608) 838-3258
www.ginakdesigns.com

Hambo Stamps
www.hambostamps.com

iLoveToCreate™
(800) 438-6226
www.ilovetocreate.com

Imagination International Inc.
(541) 684-0013
www.copicmarker.com

JustRite
(866) 405-6414
www.justritestampers.com

Kaisercraft
(888) 684-7147
www.kaisercraft.net

Karen Foster Design
(801) 451-9779
www.karenfosterdesign.com

Kraftin' Kimmie Stamps
www.kraftinkimmiestamps.com

Lil' Inker Designs
www.lilinkerdesigns.com

Lili of the Valley
www.liliofthevalley.co.uk

Lily Bee Design
(801) 820-6845
www.lilybeedesign.com

Lockhart Stamp Co.
(707) 775-4703
www.lockhartstampcompany.com

MAGNOLIA-licious
(604) 594-5188
www.magnoliastamps.us

Make it Crafty
www.makeitcrafty.com.au

Making Memories
(800) 286-5263
www.makingmemories.com

Melissa Frances
(877) 885-1261
www.melissafrances.com

Memory Box
www.memoryboxco.com

Michaels Stores Inc.
(800) MICHAELS (642-4235)
www.michaels.com

Mo's Digital Pencil
www.digitalpenciltoo.com

My Favorite Things
(352) 508-1404
www.mftstamps.com

My Mind's Eye
(800) 665-5116
www.mymindseye.com

Neenah Paper
(800) 994-5993
www.neenahpaper.com

October Afternoon
(866) 513-5553
www.octoberafternoon.com

Our Craft Lounge
(877) 44-LOUNGE (445-6864)
www.ourcraftlounge.net

Papertrey Ink
www.papertreyink.com

The Peddler's Pack Stampworks
(800) 29-STAMP (297-8267)
www.peddlerspack.com

Prima Marketing Inc.
(909) 627-5532
www.primamarketinginc.com

PrintWorks Collection Inc.
(800) 854-6558
www.printworkscollection.com

Provo Craft
(800) 937-7686
www.provocraft.com

Ranger Industries Inc.
(732) 389-3535
www.rangerink.com

Scrapper's Must Haves
www.scrappersmusthaves.com

SEI
(800) 333-3279
www.shopsei.com

Sizzix
(877) 355-4766
www.sizzix.com

Spellbinders™ Paper Arts
(888) 547-0400
www.spellbinderspaperarts.com

Stampavie
(210) 445-2672
www.stampavie.com

Stamping Bella
(866) 645-2355
www.stampingbella.com

Stampin' Up!
(800) STAMP UP (782-6787)
www.stampinup.com

Taylored Expressions
www.tayloredexpressions.com

Tiddly Inks
www.tiddlyinks.com

Tim Holtz/Advantus Corp.
(904) 482-0092
www.cropperhopper.com

Tombow USA
www.tombowusa.com

Tsukineko LLC
(425) 883-7733
www.tsukineko.com

Uchida of America Corp.
(800) 541-5877
www.marvy.com

Verve Stamps
www.shopverve.com

Whiff of Joy
www.shop.whiffofjoy.com

Whipper Snapper Designs Inc.
(262) 938-6824
www.whippersnapperdesigns.com

WorldWin Papers
(888) 843-6455
www.worldwinpapers.com

Zva Creative
(801) 243-9281
www.zvacreative.com

The Buyer's Guide listings are provided as a service to our readers and should not be considered an endorsement from this publication.